CLASSIC ROCK

Unique, Distinctive Piano Arrangements of 20 Hit Songs

ISBN 978-1-4950-0314-1

HAL•LEONARD®
CORPORATION
7777 W. BLUEMOUND RD. P.O. BOX 13819 MILWAUKEE, WI 53213

Visit Hal Leonard Online at
www.halleonard.com

ANOTHER ONE BITES THE DUST

Words and Music by
JOHN DEACON

Steady Rock

To Coda

AQUALUNG

Words and Music by IAN ANDERSON
and JENNIE ANDERSON

Moderately

BACK IN BLACK

Words and Music by ANGUS YOUNG,
MALCOLM YOUNG and BRIAN JOHNSON

Moderate Rock

15

D.S. al Coda
(no repeat)

CODA

1.

2.

ff

8vb

BARRACUDA

Words and Music by NANCY WILSON,
ANN WILSON, MICHAEL DEROSIER
and ROGER FISHER

Moderately fast

18

19

BEAST OF BURDEN

Words and Music by MICK JAGGER
and KEITH RICHARDS

23

BORN TO BE WILD

Words and Music by
MARS BONFIRE

Fast Rock

THE BOYS ARE BACK IN TOWN

Words and Music by
PHILIP PARRIS LYNOTT

Medium Swing

LAYLA

Words and Music by ERIC CLAPTON
and JIM GORDON

Moderately fast

CARRY ON WAYWARD SON

Words and Music by
KERRY LIVGREN

To Coda ⊕

44

CODA

MONEY

Words and Music by
ROGER WATERS

OWNER OF A LONELY HEART

Words and Music by TREVOR RABIN,
JON ANDERSON, CHRIS SQUIRE
and TREVOR HORN

Moderately

RADAR LOVE

Words and Music by GEORGE KOOYMANS
and BARRY HAY

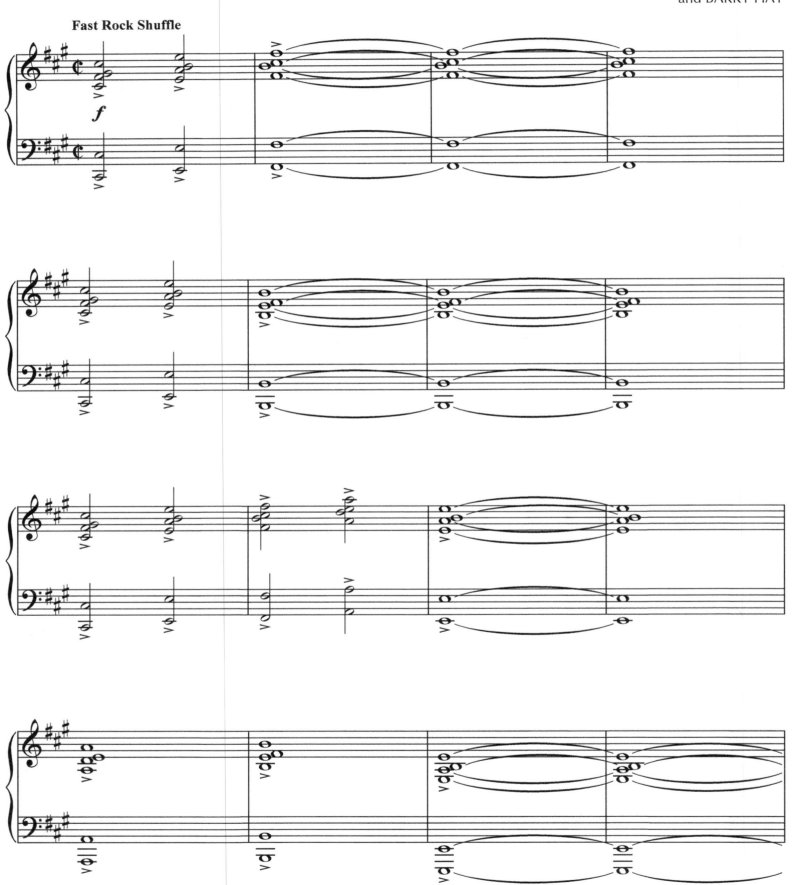

ROXANNE

Music and Lyrics by
STING

Moderately, with freedom

SWEET HOME ALABAMA

Words and Music by RONNIE VAN ZANT,
ED KING and GARY ROSSINGTON

Moderately

SMOKE ON THE WATER

Words and Music by RITCHIE BLACKMORE,
IAN GILLAN, ROGER GLOVER,
JON LORD and IAN PAICE

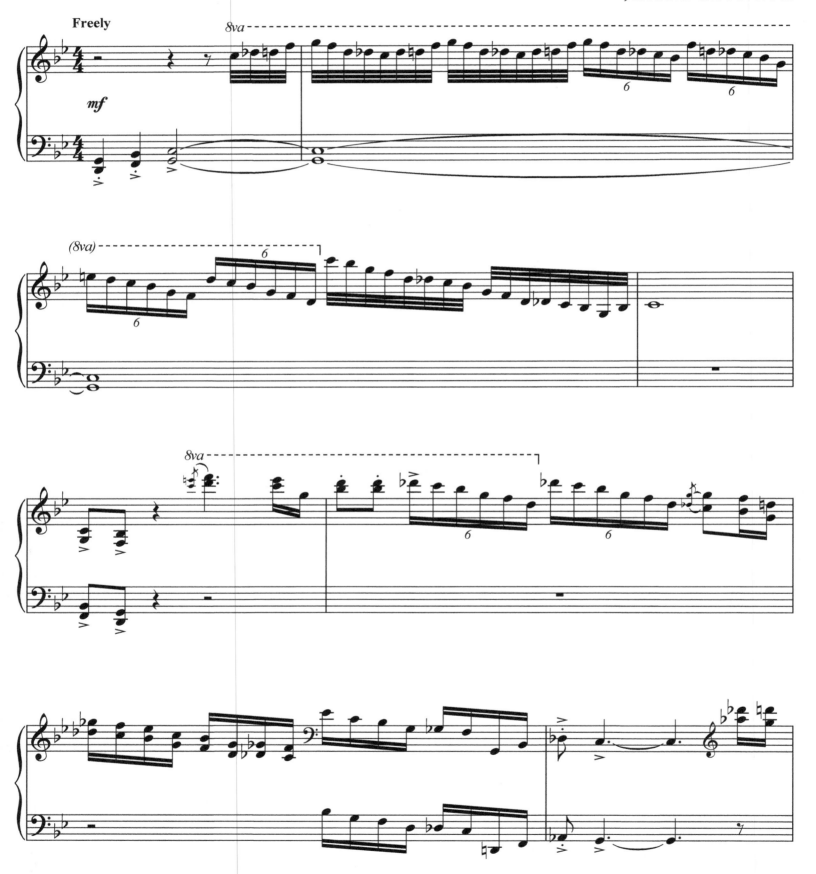

Driving Rock

SUFFRAGETTE CITY

Words and Music by
DAVID BOWIE

Tempo I

SWEET EMOTION

Words and Music by STEVEN TYLER
and TOM HAMILTON

Moderately, in 2

Depress keys silently, and hold sostenuto pedal throughout.

Release sost. pedal

TAKIN' IT TO THE STREETS

Words and Music by
MICHAEL McDONALD

25 OR 6 TO 4

Words and Music by
ROBERT LAMM

Slowly, in 2

Moderately slow, in 2

WELCOME TO THE JUNGLE

Words and Music by W. AXL ROSE,
SLASH, IZZY STRADLIN',
DUFF McKAGAN and STEVEN ADLER

Moderately fast

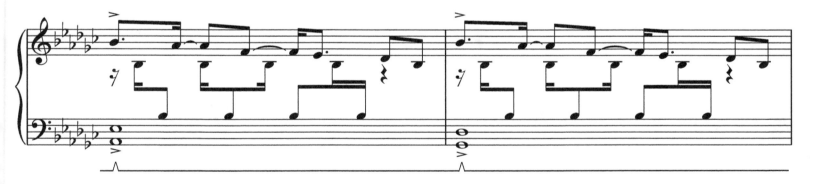

Tempo I

YOUR FAVORITE MUSIC
ARRANGED FOR PIANO SOLO

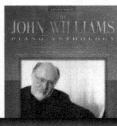

ARTIST, COMPOSER, TV & MOVIE SONGBOOKS

Adele for Piano Solo
00307585...............................$17.99

The Beatles Piano Solo
00294023...............................$17.99

A Charlie Brown Christmas
00313176...............................$17.99

Paul Cardall – The Hymns Collection
00295925...............................$24.99

Coldplay for Piano Solo
00307637...............................$17.99

Selections from Final Fantasy
00148699...............................$19.99

Alexis Ffrench – The Sheet Music Collection
00345258...............................$19.99

Game of Thrones
00199166...............................$17.99

Hamilton
00345612...............................$19.99

Hillsong Worship Favorites
00303164...............................$12.99

How to Train Your Dragon
00138210...............................$19.99

Elton John Collection
00306040...............................$22.99

La La Land
00283691...............................$14.99

John Legend Collection
00233195...............................$17.99

Les Misérables
00290271...............................$19.99

Little Women
00338470...............................$19.99

Outlander: The Series
00254460...............................$19.99

The Peanuts® Illustrated Songbook
00313178...............................$24.99

Astor Piazzolla – Piano Collection
00285510...............................$17.99

Pirates of the Caribbean – Curse of the Black Pearl
00313256...............................$19.99

Pride & Prejudice
00123854...............................$17.99

Queen
00289784...............................$19.99

John Williams Anthology
00194555...............................$24.99

George Winston Piano Solos
00306822...............................$22.99

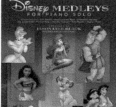

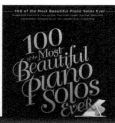
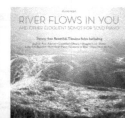

MIXED COLLECTIONS

Beautiful Piano Instrumentals
00149926...............................$16.99

Best Jazz Piano Solos Ever
00312079...............................$24.99

Best Piano Solos Ever
00242928...............................$19.99

Big Book of Classical Music
00310508...............................$19.99

Big Book of Ragtime Piano
00311749...............................$22.99

Christmas Medleys
00350572...............................$16.99

Disney Medleys
00242588...............................$17.99

Disney Piano Solos
00313128...............................$17.99

Favorite Pop Piano Solos
00312523...............................$16.99

Great Piano Solos
00311273...............................$16.99

The Greatest Video Game Music
00201767...............................$19.99

Most Relaxing Songs
00233879...............................$17.99

Movie Themes Budget Book
00289137...............................$14.99

100 of the Most Beautiful Piano Solos Ever
00102787...............................$29.99

100 Movie Songs
00102804...............................$29.99

Peaceful Piano Solos
00286009...............................$17.99

Piano Solos for All Occasions
00310964...............................$24.99

River Flows in You & Other Eloquent Songs
00123854...............................$17.99

Sunday Solos for Piano
00311272...............................$17.99

Top Hits for Piano Solo
00294635...............................$14.99

HAL•LEONARD®

View songlists online and order from your
favorite music retailer at
halleonard.com